GOD COMPLEX

T0322534

RACHAEL ALLEN

God Complex

faber

First published in 2024
by Faber & Faber Ltd
The Bindery, 51 Hatton Garden
London EC1N 8HN

Typeset by Hamish Ironside
Printed in England by Imprint Digital, Exeter

A CIP record for this book is available from the British Library

ISBN 978-0-571-37991-0

4 6 8 10 9 7 5 3

This book is for Luke

He has martyred me, but for no cause
ELIZABETH SMART

Never waste your pain
Saint Maud

I look out
through stained glass
pressing my neck
for religious lumps.
In my head, time works
on a flattened disc.

Here is a wasteland
of past aesthetics
patched up with modern tubes,
a church. Perhaps
I have a deity in me –
lucid angel in the soft reflection –

I

It's a risk, a life with someone.
The last time we saw each other as incompatible lovers
I felt a shift occur in my body,
the blood switching direction in the vein.

It was low burrs of late July,
humming day, aging sun, pollen gore.
The light behind you halo-made your head
and it was cliché.

What is it to love a person? Or a virus, a prophylactic acid?
A trouble in the systemics? Which is like a riot in the
municipal architecture of a body. How emotion and clinging
affliction make a way through sinus and back out again.

Immediately after you left, I swam in the toxic river.
Rapid and thick with hard-scummed edges,
feverish from farm waste and floating cut grass.
Algal blooms in eddying parts from
animal matter, made inorganic with antibiotics,
a clean gassy odour reminding me I'm not far from people,
or animals kept by people. I swim in the slush,
and the effluent coats me.

Red roots grow like a photograph I saw
of a Monsanto-plumped lake,
plant arms turned pink from runoff,
hemming the water, nothing else can grow
from the glyphosate.

Pursued by ciphers, congregational with herself, mad
me swam in those green mothlike fumes of evening. Sere
scenery all around. Old chemical smell of gum. I float under
the meshed structure of the sky and thank god I am grieving
while the climate dims. What an effort otherwise.

Wildflowers spotting all around – leek-green innards,
marshmallow pink – their multiple dislocating smells.
You had gone. So what if I just let the river take me
wherever it wants to. There is a disruption of fate by not
allowing rivers to do what they want.

I give the water too much agency. The river doesn't care to
take anyone anywhere; it is fated to move. I was just existing
in its movement.

Houses we rented. Rows of pebbledashed houses.
Pebbledashed walls of modernist,
overpriced council houses.
Or the homely view of the
boarded-up public toilet block
strip light flickering in the coming dusk
on the green between towering flats.

Men arrived unannounced,
rolling machines over walls to check for asbestos.
They fumbled in the old-doily drapery,
skirting peeling like an orange,
pointing, telling us not to breathe
too forcibly in that corner.

How to tell a story faithfully and to the cause?
Our first house overlooked
the bloodbath soil of a racecourse,
where the mechanics of a purebred horse leg
are oiled, machinic synchronicity.
You can see wealth in horses.

There is blood in the lungs of the racehorse
after excessive performance.
The horse starts to disembark internally
when it has leant too hard on itself.

Popcorn-ceilinged little dramas.
Arguments spreading like mould
corroding through walls,
delicate concretions of damp
a good slap colour.

No frames on the wall, no curtains.
When a friend stayed the night
she placed newspaper over the windows, embarrassed.
The newspaper remained until we left.

Twinship. A grievance, your cruelty; how much I gave away in public, and anything that felt like gossip, the maintenance of your social order. Never eating but watching. I was to steer clear of fierce opinions, flirting, house prices and inherited wealth. I'd paid for those conversations before.

We didn't hold hands or engage in public displays of affection, and when you did – the evening's going on and you're drowsy – it felt wrong, like balancing a large, dead fish on my leg, stinking and shedding scale.

At the end of such an evening, objects were thrown in a dilapidated fashion. Plastic chipping from the hair curlers I left in your room. No bleeding, silent treatment.

Sorry was the language I learned.

I followed you too far into the ill-green of your mind.
Green at an angle, grading up in colour: the darker green
of a plane's still-flying shadow on the lattice of field as it
lands. Light joins in a continuum. Frequencies occur, a flash
between my eyes.

When I stand in one position, hand to my forehead, shading
the light, I can imagine you stepping off a train and the limits
come into play: you loom larger. How can one tree's stem and
bark represent the logic and order of my own perspective?
Is a branch or a tree in this way like deep feeling,
unboundaried and usual?

What about that livid green over there? Suddenly it stands
out, an unnatural green, as if there can be such a thing. It is
back-of-chessboard or hardware-store green. The green of
a swing bin or car door. But it is planted and skew-whiff in
shapes; someone's garden of entropy, someone's flowering
bit of temple. Sorry.

Your mother standing in the doorway would tell me about
the things she did to you, *things that may explain his
behaviour*. I enjoyed being used but could not say, hand
pressed over a red-hot grate, that I enjoyed it. I make you
here the scapegoat, mimetic violence.

I lived by your mood, an operational system. Facial expressions trained in the Petri dish, your mood was a hard bound hand against me, and my hands bound hard behind me, against wood.

How overcome is the day? Between morning veils and a tendril of thought. The daily mapping of tractability, travelling through a rhizome backwards and forwards in time.

I take solace elsewhere, but the person I looked to for love is the horse's bit between my teeth; ancient dentistry or torture device. I used to look up and feel the earth come apart in my stomach with power or potential; not now, you have closed me.

The estranged blood in the vein – that's from a book.

The early days were chemical.
The first sight of you:
the childhood game of a pretend egg cracked over a head,
fist balled and hands spreading
an imagined warmth through the body.
Speech felt under water in its difference
to speech with everyone else.

A contract was being drawn up,
it became a habit to acquiesce.
Eutrophication of the body,
the taste and feel of a drying scab,
my eyes were being put out
by your spit and my duty.

It cost me
for sure
to sit alongside you.
Forced down
your food
forced down
your thinking.
I came across you
so deep in sadness,
a sadness that churned
like a river bottom
and transformed
in you
for me
as a hatred.
Ill-equipped and
nascent
I held
the apoplectic anger
for you
while you would pace and tut:
don't say this to me,
do say that.

Only I saw you divinely.
A screaming figure flailing their torso
on a concrete altar.
Pressed, mythical, with an undiagnosed condition.

First time: I gave up fighting.
A dingy house, eight bedrooms,
plywood furniture, new graduates,
theatrically mouldy, too temporary to be haunted.
You lay on top of me with your whole weight and old coat.
I said no. I had an eye infection, weeping with stress.
I paid attention to the people in other rooms,
sober, dreaming, clean. I took myself
to the chair opposite and watched.
I took and took myself to the chair.

In a hair shirt crawling through a vast and febrile state, I was learning what it meant to be subservient to someone, miraculous, the dog.

In the objects thrown, a deity chipped. Old peach-weathered fresco in the dampened church. Channels of history being brought into. I had marked times for sleeping and waking. There was scheduled haranguing, my phone phobic, cyclical. A weekend where I drank too much without you, and you ripped the hem of my shirt. I went to bed while you loomed in the doorway. I was dangling by a thread, opposite monasticism.

Compulsion of pressure in gauze tenderness. The length of your body vulnerable, with an energetic awareness of your surroundings, vibrational, like the dog. If you heard me in the kitchen, I would feel the centre of gravity shift. I knew you would be coming to find me. What does it mean to require and invite attention, like an old bad clown? I couldn't make myself small enough not to be heard.

The final house we shared was by the river,
a black water garden.
The river was deep and ran according to my moods.
When things were better, we'd walk the river.
In the summer, stop by a bar,
sitting under a parasol,
silent drinks in glasses.

Once, twice, three times a year,
the river would burst its bank.
The river would burst its muscly bank
all over the closed bars and into our house,
dark, destroying our rooms,
like someone in unpredictable rage.
The parasols and our belongings heading out to sea.

I have never kept a journal,
and this reminds me why.
I am too precarious in all directions.
I wake up even now in the night,
sweating over flooded documents.

The house belonged to a friend; it was a family spare. Itchy woollen blankets in every cupboard, unused, not thinning. Expensive things last longer; words from the rich. Candle holders of a hard, marbled quality, inheritance. The home was empty, because of the flooding river, and they needed someone there, as though bodies can warm a house, or stop water. Our possessions were ok to be flooded; they were light and chipped. Aristocracy lined the walls and we paid high rent. The landlord kept fruit in his mouth and got his children jobs in universities. Every so often he'd arrive at the house drunk, no warning, and need to stay in the library room. Fall asleep with the lights on, open-mouthed, smelling like the red wine you buy on trains, his hat over his face.

The man next door bought sixteen ducklings, rearing them to shoot. He'd ordered them online, and they came in the back of a van, in boxes punctured with airholes. I watched them circle the back garden. He tended to them and gave them special feed.

The fields were chopped and wheat was stacked into square bales. One sanitary pad floated in the river's dank. The ducks flew away as soon as they could and the man was enraged. We heard him through the walls screaming at his wife.

In living I wanted to disrupt the history of women's stories in my life, but it turned out I couldn't. History is a sequence of repeating patterns so extreme they are inescapable: I watch the way previous histories are now travelled in. They are nefarious pre-fact; they're writ:

The intention of suffering
a lived punishment I felt I deserved.
I am returning you to your former meaning,
in the dim pulpits of the churches in the towns where we lived.

One held the pale curdled hand of a saint
who was pregnant when she'd been pressed to death
by weights.
I want to switch back the blood.

A bird gags sweetly on the new green deal
as I work my way through ineffable instructions

on how to live this poor and shabby life
as performance. How to pack it, sell it?

There is masochism in a decade making out
under the quilt of an unholy government

who never seem to end, who command
the dimensions of our poorness.

We grow stunted in contaminated soil,
eking into the bloodstream, bringing

an omnipresent confusion into the social
consciousness. How wholly are we to be pressed?

Listening, always,
waiting impatient.
Now it won't be.

A bit between my teeth
you galloped me around like an animal.
Dallied pet.

Rub me between your fingers like an emulsifying scent,
or what you expect to heal you.
In being used I take great power,
I try to tell myself, on all fours,
that yes I am a god in my submission.

My fault – I want lovers to find me so attractive
they want to end my life.

This is the most flattering and lasting gift bestowed upon
the women in my history:
they were so loved it calcified bone white to hate.

I have felt it
(both the want to kill and be killed),
being so loved it turns to threat – don't tell me otherwise
– is the truest.

This is what I have come to accept.

A map of my
extended family
on the wall.
The ataraxic
names of
murdered
women glow –
a pinball game.
A lorry turns
over the body
of a daughter
and turns over again
the gothic body
of a daughter.

I work myself up, I work myself down,
I work myself all around town.
Those who know me know and
those who don't still probably do.

Sometimes I feel the edges of my teeth bleed and taste
metal in my mouth, like a big iron dick
is in there,
or is it that
I'm just bleeding
from the gums again.
I ignore symptoms like
an unreciprocated *I love you*,
sitting in the mouth,
an uncomfortable cloud, growing bigger
and sharper, the kind that covers
the sun while you swim,
the turbulence kind –
the darker-water making kind –
you can only wish it away.

Land is cruel and inhospitable as a lover,
which is why we pursue it, why we punish it.

    The sun reflecting on the water looks good and
clean, like a wedding.

    I don't feel funny, I feel wrecked
      like that painting of a ship on a bladderwracked reef,

        frozen timely and always on the verge,
      radius of cursive clouds above.

Is it
  being thrown through a window as a grown woman
thrown through a grown window as a changed man
  thrown through the grown woman, a good window?

 Or growing the limbs of dead relatives
through our throats –
conjuring a lost voice, uncannily,
  murdered by a love, branch as a tongue –

    so dig until you meet these dead
    who'll all look up at you –
     I scavenge them, part militia:
    close the ground when through.

How to have sat, as a child,
at a murderer's feet and not been murdered?

We come home when
our ankles give way

and we come down
like how a horse breaks its neck,

a bent black pipe
angled against grass.

Your large face, creamy-bulbous,
clattering through my recurring dreams
where I cling to a harbour wall
in a rough-edged sea.

A blonde girl turns in currents
at the bottom of the cliff.
Crosses in the marsh
and a low frosted mist.
I expected the worst
would happen
and it did.

                              Husband, wearily
              I admit to having these dreams –
              I turn and face you, chin in hands
                            and drive and drive
                      my thumbs into your eyes.

Around around the mulberry bush
I think of victims – you.
Around the mulberry bush the garden's fed
the bones of dew.

Over the hill, along the path
I trappeth one of three
and when I go to set him free
he cometh after me.

The air got tough, late-summer, city-air tough, nettle striving
through the pavement thick, cigarette on the old curtain
air, prayer-dense. Barbeque smoke with new clothes and
disinfectant smells, rising from the bottoms of restaurants
and mingling with the park edges. Beer sweat on a warming
sleeve all night, inner elbow. In the bathroom we ate pills
and tugged on an emblem. I became obsessed with nefarious
facts about you. I wanted parts of you inside me forever. In a
parallel universe we are still there. I was not left for someone
else but of course I was.

The seasons are slowing in their age. They fumble the order of systems, a power-mad king past his prime. The sky a collapsing tent. The river browning, chock-full of bent slurry. Time warping like a weak tree. What an embarrassment after all. I live in the timeline of clowns. *I'm not making a fool of myself for you.* In fact, you're nowhere to be seen.

Our separation moved through my body with that rough, unfamiliar blood. I lived tethered so intensely to a present moment I lost interest in myself. I had memory loss in the extreme, which adapted, became futuristic, so much so that I couldn't comprehend a time that I would want to remember, so I stopped preparing for one.

Living at the end of this country means filling up slowly
with zilch. In avenues of next doors in endless small towns,
I become uncomfortable-friendly with strangers and don't
always mean what I say. And I say a lot sitting at the bar,
bandaged, arms around a drink, chairs and tables in a row.
I am lapsed here, my hair shirt showing on the dating app.
See how I punish myself!

Gruesome melodrama with the new friends. I want to stop
taking my hormones, like an organic cow. I need metaphor
like a bird sucking at the bud, inhalation of sugar.

No such thing as something for nothing. If you know your way around one town here you know your way around them all. A country of industrial estates, ballooning from motorways like bronchioles. Churches in industrial estates. The industrial estate shaped church. The industrial estate shaped like a church. The industrial estate with the orange-rimmed church in it, stained glass in the prefab huts, and all the bodies lying in state like a reflex. The suburban dentist in their hackery. Lonely is the regional library sweating under strip light, mood spreading like a gas, flinting into oblivion. A robin there, on the bush outside, grubby from living by the hard shoulder, bloody of chest from his victims. All are living memorialisation.

I sought chaos, without understanding why, my puckered skin fraying: a ruching welt, ulcerative. I was taken to the dog park. Then you were gone. I scratched my itchy coat.

Sun-wrecked, river-slapped, useless miscellaneous. Describe the water's brown: I want a life I know I am not accessing. It lives at the bottom of this river. There is no control at any point in a narrative. Breeding swans live on the bank. I despise the lone mother bird for her freedom, weighted down by felt-grey babies with no consideration for what she can afford. Unsquashed, animals cannot be saints. *The swan is a bitch*. I took that from another book. One cygnet pokes up through white feathers, like in a Rococo painting, eyelash-tacky and colour-swept. Parenthood seems all platitude, even at the staggered nuance of the riverbank.

Poverty begets, and has this long memory, a memory stretching over me still, a film of a sunset curdling and then on pause. You are made a different colour in poverty, which is visible to everyone. In animals you should not see wealth, except you do: those pulmonary racehorses, blood curdling up in the lung.

I would imagine you and your new lover and cinematise
your lovemaking, fluorescent and air-conditioned in the way
of hotels, with plumbing that always works. Sheets changed,
out to dinner. Always bowls of chips. Cute and early bruise.

From my window, boats went by, rented for the slow
evenings, fringe-glowing the water. Hordes of men in fancy
dress drop plastic spoons and cups. Hen-do masks float
mask-side-up, feathers sprouting from the tip. This was
rat-sweetened water. It was people flavoured.

Moth-beaten. Gorge on earth, when we are hungry, or at least when starved of a very true romance. A romance that is as untrustworthy as a dune and scatters like a loose dune in even a faint wind. Glass thrown against the wall is not an indication of an occurrence of nature or what is natural; a caterpillar's gnostic face in the frost.

Observe the model of your living. I was the colour of a pale house on fire: pink at the edges. The colour of a blackened lung frozen then defrosted: pink in the middle. I would love and fuck every wall in my mania, even the ancient ones, even the Roman ones.

In this pain I was a charred donkey in an office chair – steaming, stupid and unusual. I'd have whole conversations with myself pretending half of me was you. I was so alone, so deeply, there was only river, and an inexplicable dome of smoke in the sky.

In company, I'd watch myself perform as though televised.
Alone, I watched the animated ice shelf sink into the blue
abyss. Learned about the paradise crow: inaccurate drawings
led to years of misinformation. Couldn't sleep all night, one
hour on, one hour off, synthetic light streaming through my
dreams like the smell of verdant mould.

I will be believed one day, if not for this performance,
then perhaps my next. What would happen if there was a
microphone installed somewhere in this bedroom? Yes, I too
for the life of me cannot remember what we talked about.

I dreamed so much of the building you met her in I can visualise it now. I have drawn it limply as a child recalls through drawing, naive. A metallic, institutional structure, half mixed with the concrete reality of the space I stalked online.

God damn an ex-wife! God damn a new wife! I am the equidistant route from one to the other, a tree-slut, wearing my wig and sat like a crab in the wayward ditch, a signpost. In obedience, travesty dump.

How to cart off such deep pain? Emerging from the mouth, light in all directions, built to practise offstage. Like sexual deviance. The theatre of its being is vast, lonely and without share. It is a house imposing, slanted on a hill, one rusty bucket burning on the incline, a famous painting. Symbolic and manipulative. Even to talk about grief like this proves it is all performance. *Ta-da*.

For company I look to the sheet-white sky, streaked with medicinal blues, or towards a barren tree, reaching up. The iridescence of a smell like an old man's meat on thermals, a flasher's thin stink on the air, animal scent glimpsed. Unspeakable things happen everywhere, like you, who are lilac with cold.

Desiccated cloud-aura of razored evenings, factory sky is gravied. I tip through tea-stained hallways in afternoon light, seagull barking down the chimney, worthless horror, only just leaving the house when the children return from school; dirty embarrassments of domesticity. A fool a priori, I have no convictions or degrees, just this hagiography and small island of fascist romance and identikit lanes. Walls with subsidence I pay to loan.

Now I live closer to the soil and its mineral bitterness, plugged into its data, and haunt like anyone haunts day to day. I begin to smell compromised, like a worker. I loved someone who turned me into a little frog. I try on hats in the grubby wilderness of solitude and blow up anyone who looks to inhabit the area.

Does she end up face down in pale lilac gorse? Sinking fast in a pile of suffocating grains? Is she found mouthing script in a jester's hat, clowning her pain at interview? (All of the above).

II

saints in the wild

Winter, and I arrive at a beach
I knew from childhood and think
I've been here before, more years back than I've been alive.
Confirmation there's been a lifetime already,
even stupider than this one.

Are you
done with me?
Fly in the buttercream of a plastic rose.
I stand where we first met
and am inconsolable.
The river starts moving too quickly and
the bloated strands of it all at once.
The river and the wires above it shaking like a fit
that perfectly suits my mood.
Crazed moon options in the sky
scudding in fast-mo.
Coastal grains –
solar noon.

I have a catastrophic resistance to other people
that comes after a great saturation
of feeling, adrenal failure.
I'm leaving Europe while the clouds look British.
History just goes binge purge binge purge
like me and like me its heart-busted by the river.
I'm knackered.
As knackered as the
Madonna della Misericordia,
holding all the men
through her shelter.

Weather is grey effort of collusion,
cream sky, peach lid, green stamped,
shoulder of nebular blue
crouched over or slouching
the way machinery does when stopped,
democratic and still on a Sunday.

If you feel you require a life lived in extremes, the monotony of day-to-day existence is a chore. Being lost at sea is an extreme I crave, salt on the thigh, baking wet horizon, too far out to turn back, a tugging at the calves.

A moth's thick spine
like a glitch in the vision.
Hairy gummy bear
coming over your shoulder.
If it goes in your ear
I won't tell you.

My emotions are zooed into the borehole of a tree.
Even as I look in, they are becoming extinct.
I would have had your children.
Beneficial and tempered,
marital; as water boatmen are to surface.
No really.
It's beckoning to me, this disaster horizon, walking
backwards into rain,
with only one emotional cloud.
One emotional cloud and the red outline of trees.
Price the tree's worth, that hosts a government of microbe
wet nurses,
the ones that support a sequence of systems that lean on me
(a man; a gut).

Sprinklered green lawn, peppered
blue steak, burning intensely,
like the snap of an insect combusting
in one of those restaurant machines;
the dying egg in such an insect
is its ignited inflight system.

I am keen to pick back the cuticle of the earth
and see what's underneath: fossilised insignia
of woodlouse, soft moths, embedded in old heraldry.
Loads of skin pregnant with cells, deteriorating.
History clunks on, with us clinging to the sides.

Driving as the sun banks on a kidney-shaped lake – orange spread on water – with the pine-smell swinging. The fresh, camphoraceous odour of new car spills thick on the hot plastic dash.

We see: black cows with holes in their sides, sloping their shapes like witch's capes, nuzzling the grass, an optical illusion on a riddling green. Fields are interlocking shades regimenting into purple. Heat is a trust fund sustenance.

> I am a fly on the end of your rod
> and in that moment, an indeterminate
> species, dead fly a prophecy
> in the undead mouth of a fish.

Blemish on your neck the shape and mark of a religious
burn, I did that.
I call it the worship condition.
There's a taste in my mouth
like there's a body under the tongue
all purging out like gods purged from mountains.

The rural military base on the edge
        of the beach near the shoreside
firing range. In it, red alert sounds
        in the fake suburbs built
to practise catching terrorists
        who gut real suburban homes
for their myriad developments.

The dark offshore rigs – big skeletons – look
        as though they're striding slowly
towards us, towards land.

In silence, men fight
in the old town square.
A virus skips through
blood types, plastics,
the virus skips over
kingdoms dividing
species. Splash me
nastily with science.
I would like the red
goo on my face.
I would like to
become pregnant
with this animal.

Home abortion with pineapple.
I knew with the first pain
I was sentenced. A search engine
apocryphal and winged.
My god was unnervingly resourceful.
I fell like a dog on the spike of a tree,
failed heirloom of surname heraldry,
and died fast.
The civilians of the future collapse
in tandem, like when an old spine
craves dignity, but the world gets smaller.

I pass a row of geese. I pass a Roman settlement. I pass
a crop of warm men, shirtless, in the corner of a park
playing an unidentifiable game. I pass a canal boat rotting
in the canal, stymied.

I pass a man giggling to himself in a car's reflection,
his armpit smells like carnival. Teen girls wear black and
green powder on their faces, slouching against the municipal
ridge, scheming under wrinkled spires, and the drunks, me
the best of them, in different voices, wailing lonely by the
river. I attempt to sing them the end. So much I want to
show you.

branches hold utterances

Do you ever feel like nature's bug?
Or that caterpillar's gnostic face,
or that you are being scolded by one?

Do you ever feel like nature's bastard project.
Like everyone is profiting from you.

Sense slides into oblivion.
Resentment becomes a smell stashed inside a rare flower,
only blooming once a decade, stinking as it does,
living deep in the forest of fevers.
Sky flicks through crowns
like a damaged wire.

What would I have put in the river? All the pecking-hurts that pinch in the middle of the night, when you wake up with your pants full of a stranger's innards and the air is drink-filmy with the last drop you drank before sleep, no water. You forgot to wash. Churning air is what I would call it. Anyway. Interesting what you say when someone is leaving for good.

Pain intensifies so that we remove ourselves from the source; those with such pain can travel through space and time. It is a strange form of life. I have punctured this membrane, and those who don't believe me can remain in their orbit of reality. *We'll leave you here*, they said. On the big hill. And they did. Suffering now has a purpose. But like a bug on its back, I need a little push.

The hormones I take live in the water around me and alter the water and me. Some give me migraines, some give me margins, some stop the bleeding, some start it up. The mercury revs in my veins and chambers. The fish take my drugs through the water, so I am closer to them, and their bodies begin to morph to look like mine. I giggle at them through the water with their hairy heads, *we are synced!*, I type.

I woke up certain I was pregnant with your twins, as though the logic of the universe had shifted, I was a new stranger in real normality, the old blood all flushing back. I was certain the future was not a set of unfolding planes of possibility all darker in their outlines, comic strips into the distance, in a way I could not keep track of.

Those dreamed twins move away from me and through the coastal scud, carrying each other in and out of the mire, playing, becoming silhouetted outline. I cannot catch them up. Taken by incompatible plastic names, in tertiary. Their stomach, nose and brain forms backwards.

They go to the beach, arm in arm, and I lose them for so long that they starve in the dunes. I cannot stop them dying, for they never existed anyway. When I eventually find them, I see they have been there for years, their skins receded from facade, shin bones sanded.

But then I really woke up and I was not pregnant. I woke up and again could not afford to be pregnant, could not afford the pregnancies I never allowed myself to have. Bad river pounds on. Brown swan, stuffed with babies, babies pulsing from her back. Animals are greedy mothers. Save some for me!

Pain as truth, a good, hard fish that lives on the tip of a wave, and beneath that, a much larger fish, more like a shadow, which is the reality of the situation. Pain is that fish who wears a parasite for a tongue; like how I wear you as frontispiece. Or does the parasite wear the fish, and to what enzyme do we give praise. Who's digesting who around here?

I am the small fish that eats the larger fish from the inside out, then sits in her like a pilot, jabbing with a fin, a phantom pregnancy. Like how the fly enshrines the maggot, I live for the smaller, badder bit inside me. This is the me I digest. I'll eat my way out. We did disrupt a fate.

Apparitions of horsehair from my head, stringing together to create a body out of ropes, the tapestry threads the wayward shape of splaying veins, dropping like a net to the floor, beginning to connect to the world through sisal knots, flushing grit back to the blood.

What did I pay to acquiesce to you and how do I still to your memory? I'll begin at the gas station of going home.

Change my mind. Change my jumper.
This hoop jumping catastrophising, holding hands under a
large opaque moon.
I knew we would not survive this greenly, and if we did,
creatures would make loops around our houses, confined as
anyone.

Memories are tactile, a deep entrenched old smell,
an engastration of feelings.

The skeletal rat shell of a decomposed rodent.
Is the skeleton that remains memory or is the body that is
lost one?

I know a skeletal brook
black with fern mulch, starved as me,
 that holds a sopping batch of eggs
clinging to rocks
  from a frog, fish or toad.
    How should I know? What do I care?
 The eggs keep splitting, externalised atoms, cystic.
They disintegrate like ice in a bath, ragged,
  secreting towards the open mouth
 of a tunnel built into a hill.
Gummy and translucent, edged with mucus,
 the eggs are accosted
    by the stream's natural movements,
clapping around without intention
 like how a man approaches,
or how a hand slaps water, or skin,
  in play, or not play.

I have this army
of men's brains.
What should I
do with them next.

fool's spring

A red light on a lonely boat
swings out to sea on brine waves.
Seaside poverty has its own smell, black and white,
simple and lead-laced like old Pyrex.

Kneeling on a threadbare carpet,
praying towards the dilapidated Artex.
What next, I ask, and when?

I walk to the pier,
all strung through with those
migrainous threads of swaying lights,
and imagine a god breaking through the landing
but the god is me.

I track my basic experience of living back through to the
language of sorry.
A syntax sown with apology.
I have been force-fed lack
like a goose pumped too thick in life for its wrecked liver,
made too large for its future consumption.
Grain battling down a goose's throat.
So rough and close, grain and throat, they must be lovers.

Air now is a thin-blooded replica of what air should be.
Those blamed for the most waste make the least and take
the most in. Here, at the end of motorway lines and without
trains, on a declining coast, they inhale white dust that
falls from the cladding. They think they are a drain on the
resources they create. I miss skirting boards filmed with lint,
a reality all surface, and touchy. I miss ashtrays high and
mighty, very white rolling eyeballs, and dark lacy fumbling
in the back room, TV always blaring.

Never to have written a poem about falling in love, which is much the same as moving through a sticky spring stream, the banks of which are made from oil or phosphorous substance: being uncontaminated is impossible. Is a love poem about framing? These obsessions with interface reach back in time, which is to say, the form of the past pollutes a future terrain. There is blood in my carcinogens, like alphabet soup.

You rode me like an unusual skull sleigh, like a wooden scorpion wearing reins.

In the future: snow-topped medical tents.
The bath filled with blood, stains and sticks.
Birds circling a tower like flies.
Us, nowhere to be seen.
The nightmare feeling of someone calling your name
in the witch hours and you to the sound of it,
muffle-thud, through water.

I wake up to you having beckoned me,
back turned (in the dream).
Thighs soft, clothes soft, a main road lit,
raw with potential.
The path creasing with people,
synthetic, familied,
making their way home.
You were walking away,
I lost sight of you in a crowd,
punishingly generic.

Small Christ in shit;
a fly peddles through
sky, an oil pool on that pat.
Will you come back?
No, I can bewitch an insect
with a swinging tit
but never a man.

I know that in the moment that I'm dying, you will be the person I ask for. In obedience, again, a travesty. Hormone reservoir. I think about this when I've woken from drink, frightened of what you'll tell me I've gone and done, when my nerves are attempting to Velcro with sky, when my margins are blurring. How skin meets the air, membranous, like floss.

Here, I need more words for bad: detestation. You bet, I wasn't born with you stemming from my ear to surveil me, somnambulant, like a myth, or the bad twin, a growth or a drone: so I can continue without you, a budding in the vessels forcibly wrenched from the head.

Seagulls underlit by sundown.
What's the point of all this text?
I still have to live without you.
I watch people who block
the ants' nests' swirl outside
their homes. What kind of god
complex is this? Let them live;
let them maul the house
and surfaces with black trail.
Deify them and their paths.
I want an insect for a saint.

The smell of burning basil, the slip between lips in the light.
Looking up as I cycle by
a woman opposite me on the path, walking her dog, looks at
me suspicious,
wearing a mask of my face.
I think I know her, perhaps I do.

When I hear myself reading my own poems
I go deaf in one ear
cycling the path
(what's that line I forgot)
a body existing outside its outline.

                  I called the wrong thing love for so long
                  I cannot switch it back.

The tops of clouds look like waves.
Horizon a red-rimmed eye.
The synchronic in nature is carnal and veiny.
We shouldn't always write to please.

A system of Botoxed musculature, similar
to your old system, but different to a young face,
an uncanny versioning.
We will shadow each other our whole lives.

Human predilection to love the enemy
took me up to your feet like tidal trash
bubbling on the froth.

The capacity to change scene
to up and leave always.
I clutch aspects of grass in my hands
and unspool and unspool.

I with the inclement sense of time and waste
all shipped to me across ancient road-routes and seas.
I rise with time clogging in me
but am growing –

The fibrous circuitry of veins
is a council in my body –
a sequence of fraying sects
created for the processes
that gouge away without permission,
making me better.

There is a big light turned on
in there.
It gapes through my mouth
when I open it, in servitude.

Seed-colour sky, rigid altarpiece sky,
gold in the polyptych mottles.
Even more bloodletting,
these are my acts of devotion.

Seasons later, she walks in mulchy leaves, feels the first flicker of the sane, new blood. The dark field obscures her, but she'll be waving *hello*. Someone takes in night air settling on high wheat. See love move as a virus, altering preposterously, sun-dappled scenery. There she goes walking.

Acknowledgements

Thank you always to my mum, dad and sister.

This book would not exist without the collaboration and inspiration of the artists I have worked with over the last five years. Thank you Aled Simons, Ben Sanderson, Jet Swan, JocJonJosch and Sophie Ruigrok. Thank you for the continued support of Guy Robertson, Hannah Barry, Eva LeWitt, Marina Mahler, Tommaso Faraci and everyone at the Mahler & LeWitt Studios. Thank you to my colleagues, authors and students at Granta and Queen Mary; your thinking propels me. Thank you to Manchester University for an Anthony Burgess Fellowship in 2019, the space where this book began. Thank you to the Society of Authors for a grant to support the writing of this book.

The epigraphs are taken from *By Grand Central Station I Sat Down and Wept* by Elizabeth Smart and *Saint Maud*, written and directed by Rose Glass. The phrase 'the estranged blood in the vein' is taken from J. H. Prynne's poem 'Sun Set 4.56', from *Brass* (1971). The phrase 'I'm not making a fool of myself for you' is taken from W. S. Graham's poem 'What is the Language Using Us for?'. The phrase 'The swan is a bitch' is taken from Lyn Hejinian's *My Life*. The phrase 'circuitry of veins' is taken from Sylvia Legris's collection of the same name.

Thank you to the editors of publications where earlier versions of these poems appeared: *The Stinging Fly*, *The Poetry Review*, *Five Dials* and *Altered States*.

Thank you always and in most love to Harriet Moore. Thank you to the family at Faber: Matthew Hollis, Lavinia Singer, Jane Feaver, Kate Burton, Hannah Marshall, Hamish Ironside and the myriad other people whose labour makes a book a physical thing. Thank you to my friends who looked at versions of this book: Anthony Anaxagorou, Eleanor Chandler, Jack Underwood, Jesse Darling, Max Porter, Peter Gizzi, Rebecca Tamás, Sophie Collins, Sylvia Legris, Thomas Hutton, Wayne Holloway-Smith and Will Harris.

To Luna and to Rory, who I love, and to Luke; all my poems are yours, but these ones especially.